# Welcome to I'm Hungry!

Are you hungry?

There's pasta, ice cream, oranges, and beans...

Read on!

Talk About It!

# I'm Hungry!

The foods we eat grow in many ways. Food can grow on trees, vines, or in the ground.

**Word Bank**

Here are some words that you may hear or read this week:

**chocolate**
**thought (n.)**
**quietly**
**fruit**
**travel**
**gather**
**ripe**
**sort (v.)**
**soak**
**seal (v.)**

apples

tomatoes

potatoes

**Do you know how some of your favorite foods grow?**

Language Builder

# The Garden by the Sea

My family likes tomatoes.
They also like potatoes.
We *grow* them together
In the garden by the *sea*.

The fruit turns **ripe** in the fall;
So we go there with our *pails*.
We **gather** it together
In the garden by the sea.

We **sort** the *food* on Friday,
And **seal** it in cans by Monday.
We like to work together
In the garden by the sea.

# Hungry, Hungry Jack

Jack was very hungry. Dad was cooking things to eat.

"How many potatoes do you want to eat?" he asked.

Jack just thought. He thought very hungry thoughts.

Maybe one potato, thought Jack. Then fries and ice cream.

Or two potatoes with three fish sticks and baked beans.

He thought some more. How about four big baked potatoes? Then he would eat spaghetti, chips, and a cola.

**dip:** to put a little bit of something in a cup or glass

**sherbet:** frozen dessert of fruit and milk

Then maybe six apples and seven bananas with cream.

Jack could smell dinner in the kitchen.

No, maybe he would have nine burgers with ten burger buns. The last bun he would **dip** in a big cup of chocolate milk.

After that, maybe lots of nice lime **sherbet**.

Suddenly Dad called.

"JACK! How many potatoes do you want for your dinner?"

Jack felt very sick.

"Just one potato, please," he said quietly.

# From the Tree to You

Many people eat oranges. This fruit tastes sweet. It is good for you.

Oranges are grown on farms. Then they travel to you. Here is how they go from the farm to your table.

Oranges grow on trees. The trees need a lot of warm sun to make oranges.

After many days, the oranges are ready.

Workers pick the oranges from the trees. The workers gather the fruit by hand. They put it on big trucks. The trucks take the oranges to big buildings.

Inside the buildings, the oranges are washed and dried. A machine then puts them in groups. Then, the oranges are packed into boxes. Trucks take the boxes to food stores. At the store, you buy the oranges. Their trip to you is over!

# Baked Beans

Baked beans are made from haricot (HAR ee koh) beans. The beans grow in **pods** on the plants.

**pods:** parts of some plants that hold seeds

**factory:** place where things are made

The beans are picked when they are ripe. The beans are taken to a **factory**. At the factory, they will be made into baked beans.

First, the beans are sorted by size and color. Then they are washed.

1

Next the beans are soaked in hot water. This makes them soft. Then tomato sauce is made. The beans are put into cans. Then tomato sauce is poured into the cans.

2

3

Next, the beans are sealed in the cans. The cans are heated and then cooled. Finally, the baked beans are ready to go to the stores.

4

Baked beans are good for you. They help you run fast and work hard. Baked beans are very easy to cook. You just heat them up!

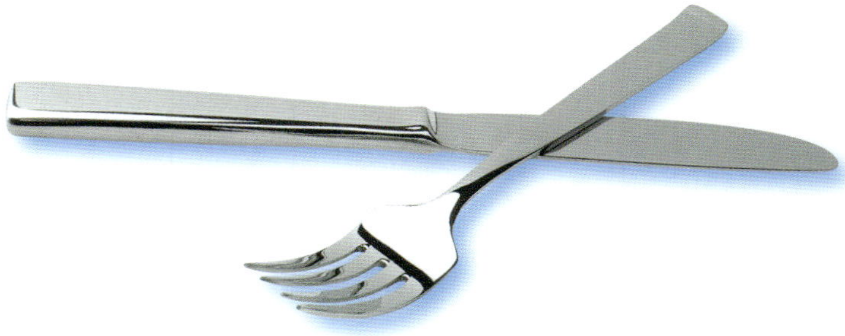

My Turn to Write

# How to Make a Sandwich

What do you need to make a sandwich you like? How do you make it? Write on pages 116 and 117 of your Studio Log.

Your notes may look like this.

**Sandwich**

ham and cheese

**What I Need**

bread
ham
cheese
tomato
mayo

**How to make it**

put mayo on the bread
add ham, cheese, and tomato
put a slice of bread on top

Your paragraph may look like this.

I like to make ham and cheese sandwiches. I need bread, ham, cheese, tomato, and mayo to make this sandwich. First I put mayo on the bread. Then I put ham, cheese, and tomato on top of the mayo. Last I put a slice of bread on top. It tastes great!

Fluency

# People Love Pasta

Pasta is a fun food. It comes in lots of shapes.

Pasta can look like strings.

Pasta can be long and flat.

Pasta can be round, too.

Some pasta even looks like shells!

Some people eat pasta with tomatoes.

That dish is fun to eat.

The tomatoes run off the pasta!

The pasta runs off the fork!

The pasta runs off the plate!

What pasta dish do you like?

Project

# A New Summer Drink

You and a friend have made a new fruit drink. Work with a partner to make a label for the new fruit drink bottle. Turn to page 118 in your Studio Log.

ISBN 1-4190-2056-0

9 781419 020568 90000

Steck Vaughn™
A Harcourt Achieve Imprint

Steck-Vaughn Summer Studio Reading